The Games Went On!

By Sandra Widener

For many years, black baseball players could not play on teams with white players. They still played baseball, though. As you read, think about how these black players handled these hard times.

PEARSON

Contents

Play Ball!	3
Black Baseball Is Born	6
Leagues Start to Form	9
The Best Years	12
Segregation Ends	21
Glossary	24
Talk About It!	inside back cover

Play Ball!

Fans cheer as New York Yankee Derek Jeter makes an amazing play. A few decades ago, though, Jeter could not have played baseball in the major **leagues**. He couldn't have played because his father is African American.

Black players could not play with white players for many years. They could only play on teams with black players. Many of these teams were part of the Negro **Leagues**.

🟧 Americans began playing baseball in the 1840s. Baseball may have come from a game called rounders. In this English children's game, a batter hits the ball. Then the batter runs around four posts, like bases.

🟢 Baseball in the 1860s was more like baseball today. Many clubs formed teams. Players paid money to join the clubs.

🟧 Many soldiers played baseball during the Civil War, from 1861 to 1865.

🟧 Teams started traveling to play each other. The players got better and better. The first **professional** team started in 1869. Players were paid for each game.

🟢 Nine more **professional** teams started by 1871. These teams had a few black players at first. That changed in the 1890s. The teams stopped hiring black players.

🟢 Some early professional teams had black players. The man circled played on this team in 1885.

Black Baseball Is Born

Baseball became more **segregated**. Black players began to form their own teams. Some black teams played against some white teams. Other white teams did not want to play against black teams.

Black teams formed in cities where many black people lived. These cities were mostly in the South and the East.

This black team played around 1890.

The Baltimore Blues Base-ball Club.

The Cuban Giants played from 1885 to 1899.

Many early black teams were called the Giants. That was because a well-known team in New York had that name. There were at least eight black teams called the Giants.

One professional black team was the Cuban Giants. The team's players weren't from Cuba. They were from New York. Some players had been on white teams. That was before baseball became **segregated**.

🟧 Early black teams often put together games on their own. Teams rode from town to town in buses and trains. They would search for other teams to play. Some teams played as many as three games a day.

🟢 Teams tried many ways to get fans. One team rode on bikes to sell tickets. Others had parades with bands. They would march to the baseball field. People would follow. Then teams would sell tickets to the game.

🟧 Teams spent hours traveling across the country to play. Posters helped spread the word about the games.

Leagues Start to Form

The first all-black baseball league was started in 1920. Andrew "Rube" Foster started the Negro National League. It had eight teams. All but one of the team owners were black. Each team paid $500 to join the league.

The league was a big hit right away. They often would have 10,000 fans at a game. That was a lot of fans for the time!

RUBE FOSTER

Foster is circled in the picture below. He owned and managed the Chicago American Giants.

🔶 In 1923, another league formed. With two leagues, there could now be a World **Series**. The best team from each league played in the series.

🟢 Another black league formed in the South. This league had a hard time for two reasons. The South was poorer than the North. There were also different laws in the South. These laws said black teams couldn't play against white teams.

🟢 The first Negro League World **Series** was in 1924.

🟨 It was hard to keep the black leagues going. One of the leagues broke up in 1928. Many teams also broke up. In 1929, the Great Depression began. Times were very hard in America. Many people lost their jobs.

🟢 Bad times also hit black baseball. Fans didn't have money to buy tickets. All the black leagues went out of business. Teams still played, though.

The Best Years

Some black teams had little money because of the Depression. That meant that owners with money could hire the best players. Two of the richest owners in the early 1930s were in Pittsburgh.

The two teams were the Grays and the Crawfords. Both had great players. But many of the best players joined the Crawfords.

The Crawfords had their own bus. The owner also built the team a place to play.

🟢 The East-West All-Star games were held from 1933 to 1950. The stands were always packed.

🔶 In 1933, a new Negro National League was formed. It was started by the owner of the Crawfords, Gus Greenlee. Another league began in 1937. Its teams were mainly from the Midwest and the South.

🟢 There were no black World Series games for many years. The biggest game each year was the East-West All-Star game. Fans voted for which players would play in the game.

🟨 The Great Depression ended in the early 1940s. About the same time America entered World War II. For black people, there were more jobs and more money. That meant good times for black baseball. There were more teams. More people went to the games. Now, players could make a fairly good living just playing baseball.

🟢 Many of the black players were great players. They were known to both black and white fans. These players would have been great in the major leagues.

🟨 Crowds filled the stands during this game in 1942. The New York Black Yankees played the Chicago American Giants in Yankee Stadium.

🔶 **Josh Gibson** There are many stories of how Josh Gibson started playing in pro baseball in 1930. One story is that a coach for a black pro team saw Gibson play on a semi-pro team. Semi-pro means the players were paid some money, but not much. One day soon after, a pro player got hurt. The coach sent a cab for Gibson who was playing across town. He left on the spot and joined the pro game.

🟢 Gibson often smashed balls into the stands. "He hits the ball a mile!" That's what a famous white pitcher once said about Josh Gibson.

JOSH GIBSON

Josh Gibson, running, played for the Homestead Grays. He played for this team for most of his career.

Gibson quickly became known for his hitting. In one game, he smashed a 500-foot home run. He hit almost 800 home runs in his career. He would have been a star in the white major leagues.

Gibson played for seventeen seasons. He died in 1947. He was only thirty-five. History was made three months later. The first black man played in the major leagues. Gibson was elected to the Baseball Hall of Fame in 1972.

🟨 James "Cool Papa" Bell

Many people think that Cool Papa Bell was the fastest runner ever to play professional baseball. A fellow player told stories about Bell's speed. He said Bell could turn off the light switch and run back to bed before the room was dark. He became a **legend**.

🟢 People said that Bell could run the bases in twelve seconds. He stole 175 bases in 200 games one season. The major league record is 130 in 162 games in one season. Bell is a **legend** for good reasons.

COOL PAPA BELL

🟨 James Bell grew up playing baseball with friends. After high school, he got a job. He also played baseball with semi-pro clubs. Bell started playing professional baseball when he was nineteen, in 1922.

🟢 A major league team asked Bell to play in 1951. Bell was forty-eight years old. He said he was too old. He never played in the major leagues. Bell was elected to the Baseball Hall of Fame in 1974.

🟨 Cool Papa Bell was a fast runner. Here, he is sliding into third base.

🟧 Leroy "Satchel" Paige

One of the best pitchers ever, black or white, was Satchel Paige. He was known for naming his pitches. A hitter might face the "bee ball," the "trouble ball," or the "hurry-up ball." He was so sure that he would strike out batters that he would sometimes tell the outfielders to sit down.

SATCHEL PAIGE

🟢 Paige was the best-paid pitcher in the Negro Leagues. Fans packed into games to see him. Paige also ran his own team. His team was called Satchel Paige's All-Stars.

🟢 Satchel Paige, circled, stands with his All-Star team. They flew to games in the team plane.

19

🟨 In 1948, Paige joined the major league Cleveland Indians. He was forty-two. Paige was the oldest "rookie" in the major leagues. A rookie is someone having his first year in the major leagues. His pitching helped Cleveland win the World Series that year.

🟢 Paige played for major league teams for several years. He also played on black teams. He pitched three innings in a major league game in 1965. He was fifty-nine. He was the oldest man to play in a major league game. In 1971, Paige was the first Negro Leagues player elected to the Hall of Fame.

🟨 Fans enjoyed watching the unusual way Satchel Paige pitched.

Segregation Ends

Black soldiers fought alongside white soldiers during World War II. That helped change the feelings of many white people toward black people. The United States started to become more **integrated.**

Branch Rickey ran the major league Brooklyn Dodgers. He thought the major leagues should become more **integrated**. Rickey hired Jackie Robinson in 1947. Robinson had been playing for a black Kansas City team.

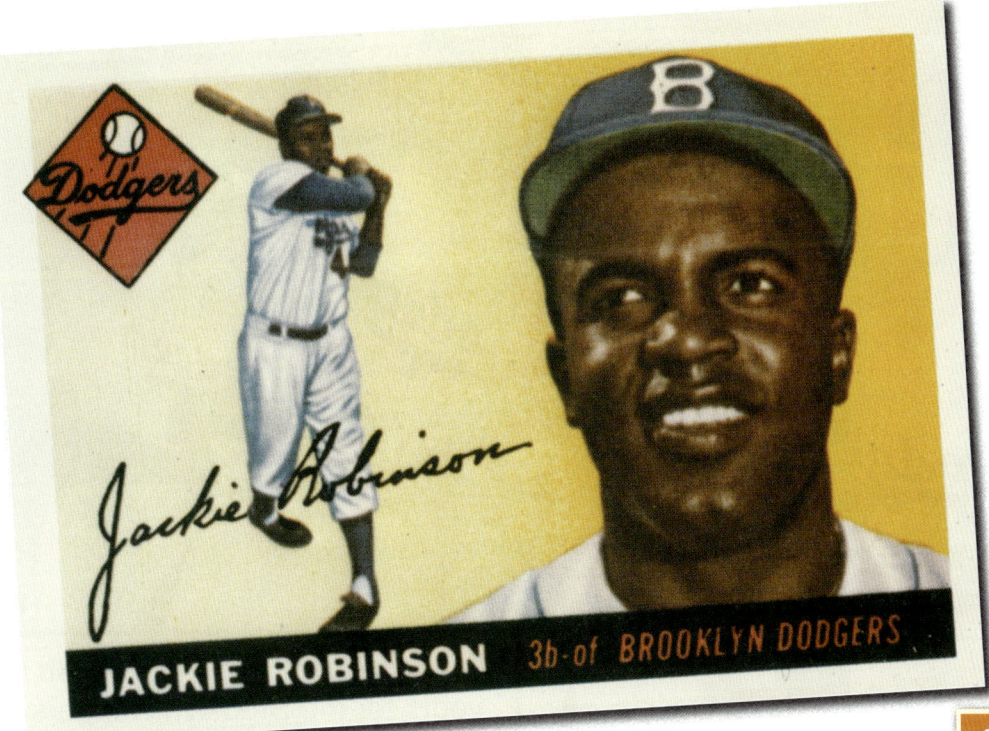

🔶 Robinson had a hard time at first. Some players and fans did welcome him. But some players would not play with him. Some pitchers hit him with pitches. Even so, he played very well. Robinson was voted the Rookie of the Year.

🟢 More black players joined the major leagues after that. That meant many of the best players left the Negro Leagues. Black fans began to go to major league games. Fewer people went to Negro League games.

🟢 Jackie Robinson played ten years for the Brooklyn Dodgers. He is in the Hall of Fame.

🟫 Soon, black baseball teams went out of business. The days of segregated baseball were over. Baseball truly became a national sport.

🟢 Now, major league players are from all over the world. It doesn't matter what color a player's skin is. What matters is how well he plays.

🟫 Today, major league players are black and white. They also come from places like Japan and Mexico.

Glossary

integrated open to all kinds of people

leagues groups of people working together to do something like play baseball

legend a remarkable person much talked about when alive and after his or her death

professional earning a living by doing something like playing a sport

segregated keeping people of different groups apart

series a number of similar things coming one after another